PLUMBER MCQ

OBJECTIVE QUESTION ANSWERS

MANOJ DOLE

Digitization is the need of the time. In the future, training in industrial training institutes will need to be conducted using online internet to make training more convenient and easy. E-books containing a set of MCQ questions will be made available to the trainees as they need to be more accustomed to the multiple choice questions MCQ to prepare for the online exams taking place in their industrial training institutes.

With all these factors in mind, Mr. Manoj Madhukar Dole Instructor, Industrial Training Institute, Satara, has written books according to the new annual system and NSQF-5 syllabus. And they've created theoretical mobile apps and blogs to make training easier, and made all these educational materials available for download on the world famous websites Google Play Store, Amazon and Apple Book Store.

The books were published by Hon'ble Joint Director Shri Rajendra Ghume Saheb Regional Office of Vocational Education and Training, Pune on 9/1/2019, at this time Shri Prakash Saigavkar Saheb Principal Government Industrial Training Institute Aundh Pune, Shri Tukaram Misal Saheb Principal Govt. Q. Sanstha Satara, Shri Sachin Dhumal Saheb District Vocational Education and Training Officer Satara, Shri Yatin Pargaonkar Saheb Principal Govt. Q. Sanstha Kolhapur, Shri Vikas Teke Saheb Inspector Vocational Education and Training Regional Office Pune, Palekar Foods Products Pvt. Ltd. Entrepreneurial Chairman of Satara Mr. Nilkanthrao Palekar Saheb, Chairman of Hira Foods Mr. Ibrahim Baba Tamboli Saheb, Mrs. Shalmali Pawar Headmaster Government Technical School Center Satara and other dignitaries were present on the occasion.

Contents

Prologue

Plumber MCQ is a simple Book for ITI & Engineering Course Plumber, Revised NSQF Syllabus, It contains objective questions with underlined & bold correct answers MCQ covering all topics including all about the latest & Important about basic fitting in the beginning and the candidate imparted training on allied trades viz., carpenter, Welding (Gas & Arc), Masonry which leads to multi-skilling. In the basic fitting the skills imparted are marking, sawing, chipping, filing, measurement, soldering, brazing, drilling, grinding and observation of all safety aspects is mandatory. The accuracy achieved is of ±0.25 mm. The safety aspects covers components like OSH&E, PPE, Fire extinguisher, First Aid etc. Cutting Pipes in different angle. Joining of pipes of different diameter and angles by gas welding, thread cutting on different types of

pipes & fittings accessories. Making of brick wall and RCC casting. Brick wall cutting for concealing pipe line. Bending of Pipes, Making of pipe line circuit for water distribution, fixing Cocks & valve, Water analysis test, Water Pressure test are being taught. alignment and laying of humed asbestos pipeline & maintenance of drainage pipe line. Installation and maintenance of Electric pumps, Construction of inspection chamber, manhole, gutter, septic tank, socket etc. Testing of drainage pipe , Removal of leakage pipe line, Installation, fixing & maintenance of valve & cock, water meter, Fixtures, hot & cold water pipe line, Repairing & reconditioning of waste pipe line, Repairing & reconditioning, scraping & painting of sanitary fittings and lots more.

We add new question answers with each new version. Please email us in case of any errors/omissions. This is arguably the largest and best Book for All engineering multiple choice questions and answers.

As a student you can use it for your exam prep. This Book is also useful for professors to refresh material.

Foreword

Vocational education and training is imparted through the Department of Vocational Education and Training through the Department of Business Education and Business Practical to supply multi-skilled artisans in line with the rapidly growing demand in the industrial sector in the 21st century. All the occupations within the institutions are important, as the trainees from these occupations develop multi-skills as per the demands of the industry.

with the noble intention of making available MCQ e-books suitable for all businesses, considering that all the examinations in all the industries in the industrial sector are conducted online and include MCQ method questions. Mr. Manoj Madhukar Dole has written a very good e-book on MCQ method as per the new annual syllabus. This e-book will definitely be a guide for all the trainees, trainee candidates, training instructors and others concerned.

The author of the book is Mr. Manoj Madhukar Dole, Instructor Gov. ITI Satara has 17 years of training experience. Written as a new annual pattern, this e-book incorporates modern digital QR Code technology to understand the layout, simple language, and simple syntax, diagrams and videos for each subject. So I am sure that this e-book will definitely be useful for in-depth study and exam practice. The work they have done is certainly commendable.

Mr. Tukaram Misal
Principal Government Industrial Training Institute Satara.

Preface

DGET New Delhi and CSTARI Kolkata have been implementing an annual pattern for all businesses in ITI since the August 2018 session. The examination system will also be changed and it will be online from this year and since all the questions are of Objective Type (MCQ), the trainees are in dire need of in-depth study. It is with this in mind that we are delighted to present the books based on the old NIMI pattern and a complete overview of the new annual pattern, and we hope that these books will be a guide for all business directors and trainees. Is.

For writing these books, Johar Awate Saheb, Principal of ITI Akluj. Former Principal of ITI Satara Saigavkar Saheb, Assistant Director Shri Chandrakant Dhekne Saheb Regional Office of Vocational Education and Training, Pune, District Vocational Education and Training Officer Sachin Dhumal Saheb and Headmaster Government Technical School Kendra Shalmali Pawar Madam and son Adhiraj Dole, mother Kusum Dole, I am very grateful to my father Madhukar Dole and wife Ashwini Dole for their special guidance and cooperation from time to time.

Also, in a very short period of time, the book was reviewed by Shri Rajendra Ghume Saheb, Joint Director, Vocational Education and Training Regional Office, Pune, for his invaluable time in publishing the book. I am sincerely grateful for their feedback.

I am grateful to the Instructor of ITI Satara for there continuous support from the very beginning of writing the book.

From this book, I consider myself blessed to have shared my thoughts on e-learning with you. I will not claim that this book is perfect, because considering the perfection, this book is an attempt and is in its infancy. They will be valuable for improvement if they are tested and suggested.

Manoj Dole
Dated 9/1/2019

Acknowledgements

The industrial training and theoretical examination system of our industrial training institutes and these changes have been accepted by the craft instructors and the trainees. Theoretical examinations conducted in your industrial training institutes are also conducted online. Since these examinations are of multiple choice MCQ method, the trainees will need to get more practice of such questions.

With all these considerations in mind, Mr. Manoj Madhukar, Director, Dole Crafts, Katari Industrial Training Institute, Satara, has done a thorough study and with his diligent work and added his keen intellect, according to the new annual system and NSQF-5 syllabus, e-book of Katari and other machine trades. -Book) and they have created mobile apps and blogs on theoretical topics to make training easier and have made all these educational materials available for download on the world famous websites Google Play Store, Amazon and Apple Book Store. Training has been made easier by creating a print version and using advanced techniques like QR Code.

All these educational materials will definitely be a guide for all the trainees for in-depth study and for the craft instructors and other concerned who are imparting vocational training.

Plumber QR Code Images

Download App
Online Test Exam
ITI Books
AutoCAD CAM
JOB & Apprentice
Online Theory
Computer Course
Trading Course
CNC Course
MSCIT Course
Shopping Business
Internet Business
Web Designing
Online Services
Top Sportsmans
Indian Army
Freedom Fighters
Top Scientists
Social Reformers
Motivational Speaker
Top Richest People
Join WhatsApp Group
Join Facebook Group
Like Facebook Page
PAN / Adhar / Licence Passport

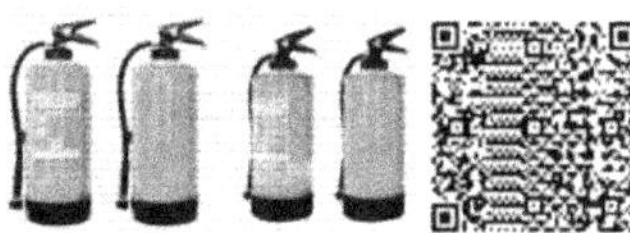

Fire extinguisher

Calliper

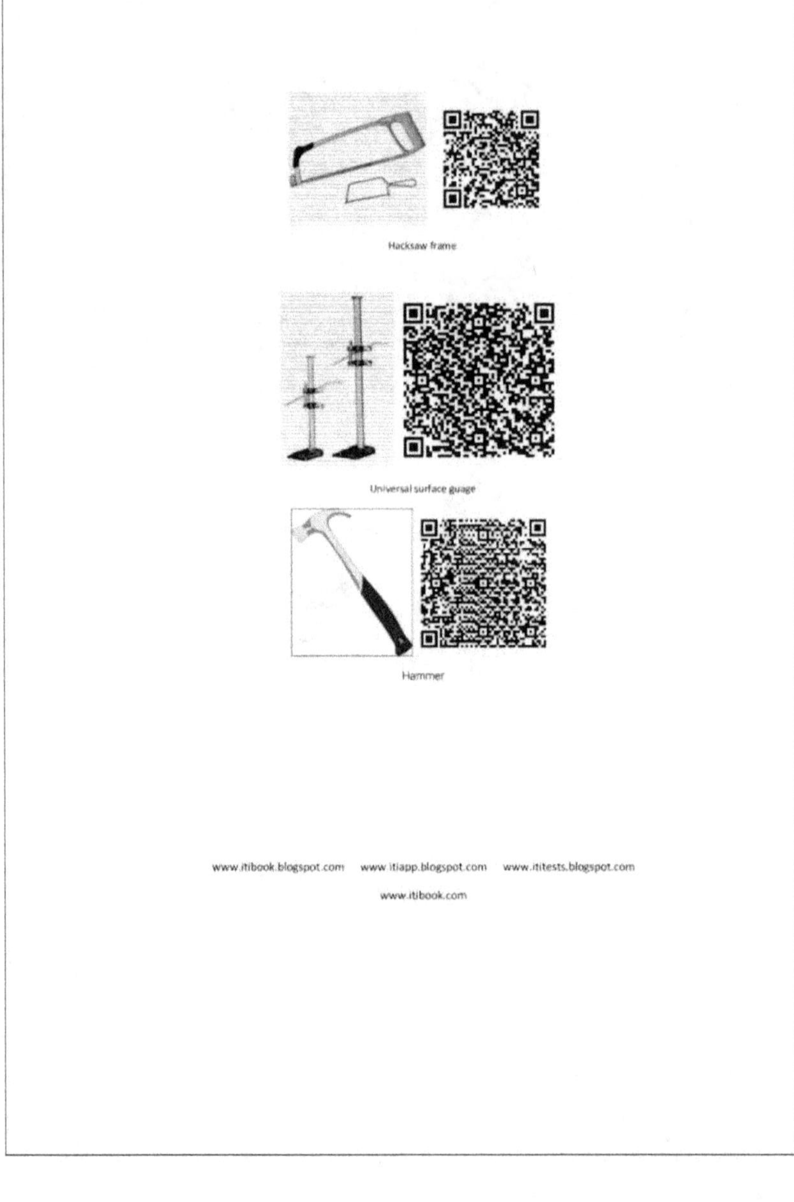

Hacksaw frame

Universal surface guage

Hammer

Centre punch

Bench vice

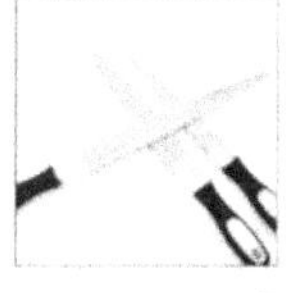

Files

Workshop Tools
drill
pipe wrench
monkey wrench
clamp
chisel
anvil
wrench / spanner
shears
ruler
adhesive tape
measuring tape
drill bit
sandpaper
paint brush
toolbox
hacksaw
nail
saw
spirit level
awl
extension cord
hammer
screw
circular saw
screwdriver
chain saw
mallet
glue
file
pliers

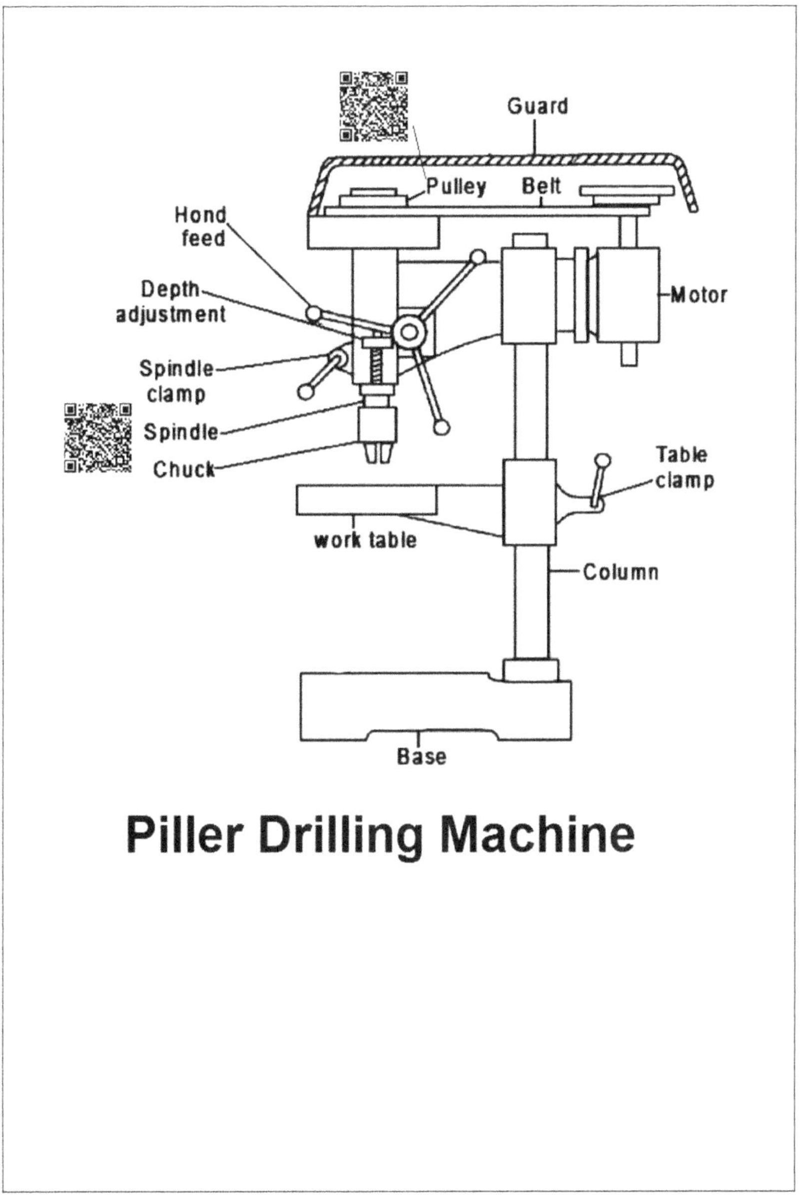

Piller Drilling Machine

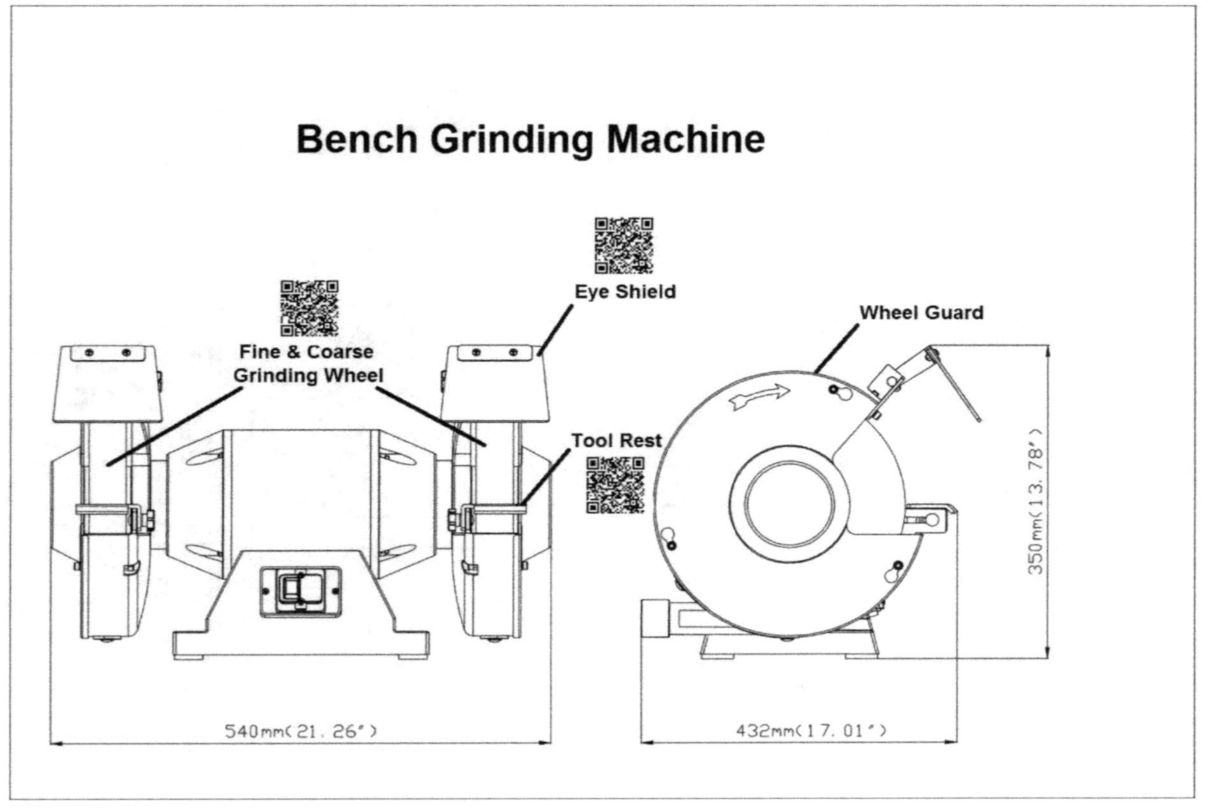
Bench Grinding Machine
Fine & Coarse Grinding Wheel
Eye Shield
Tool Rest
Wheel Guard
540mm(21. 26″)
432mm(17. 01″)
350mm(13. 78″)

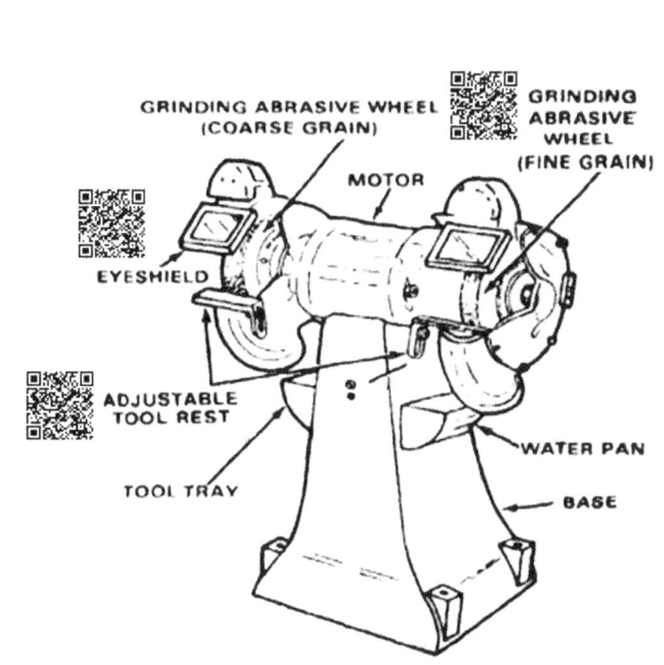

Pedastal Grinding Machine

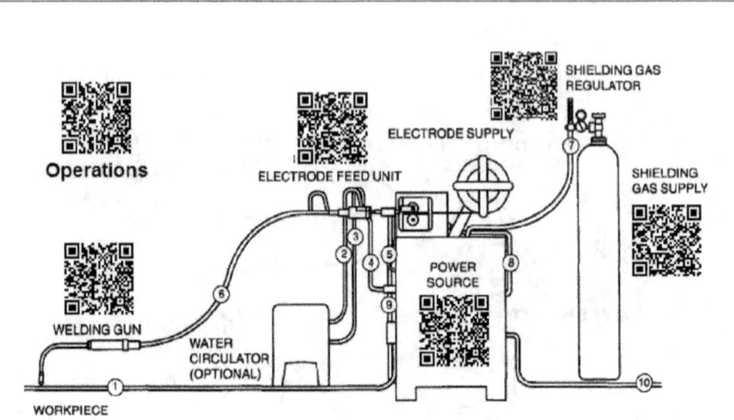

Gas Metal Arc Welding

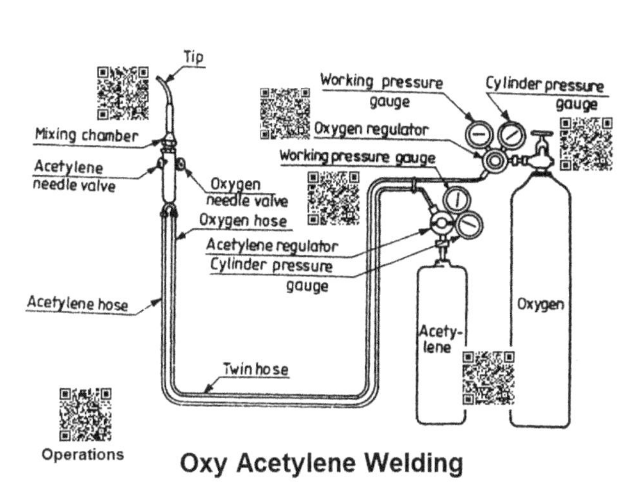

Oxy Acetylene Welding

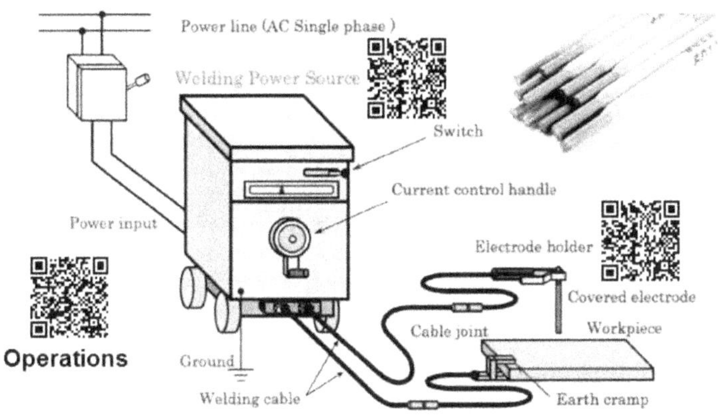

Shielded Metal Arc Welding

Plumber MCQ

1] Which one is a workshop safety?

A] Keep shop floor clean and free from grease, oil or other slippery materials

B] Stop the machine before changing the speed

C] Don't use cracked or chipped tools

D] Don't try to stop a running machine with hand

2] In Personal Protect Equipment (PPE] HELMET is used to

A] protect head

B] Protect eyes

C] Protect hands

D] Protect ears

3] Which of the following belongs to general safety?

A Have a worker in good attitude

B] The work clean and clear

C] Concentrate on your work

D] Keep the floor and gangways clean and clear

4] While grinding, which is used to protect the eyes?

A] Dark green glass

B] Mask

C] Sun glasses

D] Safety goggles

5] Which of the following is done for machine safety?

A] Check the oil level before starting the machine

B] Do things in a methodical way

C] Keep the floor and gangways clean and clear

D] Don't use dies and scarves

6] In Personal Protect Equipment (PPE], 'sleeves' is used to protect

----

A] Face
B] Eyes
C] Ears
D] Hands
7] ABC stands for --------------
A] Automatic Breathing Control
B] Automatic Blood Control
C] Airway Breathing Circulation
D] Automatic Blood Circulation
8] Fire & FIRE EXTINGUISHERS

Fire extinguisher

9] To put off"Class B" fire, the types of fire extinguisher used is ....
A] dry power
B] Carbon dioxide
C] Jet of water
D] Foam type
10] Which type of fire extinguisher is used to put off general fire?
A] Water type Extinguisher
B] Foam type Extinguisher
C] Dry chemical powder Extinguisher
D] Carbon dioxide (C02] Extinguisher
11] In case of bleeding, take treatment Of
D] cold 3" and rest
A] spray cold water
B] Bandage immediately -----.
B] Enquire about the accident thought treatment

12] in case of an accident, the victim should im
A] Asked to take rest
C] Attended immediately
D] leave him
13] First aid is given to an injured or ill person primarily....
A] Save life
B] Prevent further deterioration of the muff's
C] Give best possible comfort
D] All of these
14] Colour code for Bins for waste paper segregation is -----
A] blue Colour
B] Yellow Colour
C] Red Colour
D] Green Colour
15] In Japanese Seiko stands for --------------
A] Shine
B] Sort
C] Standardize
D] Sustain
16] Benefit of SS system is ------
A] Increase in productivity
B] Increase in quality
C] Reduction in wastage of time
D] All of these
17] Safety is -----------
A] nobody's business
B] every bodise business
C] Some bodies business
D] The organization business
18] For basic categories of safety signs are available The meaning of"prohibition" sign ----

A] shows it must not be done
B] Shows what must be done
C] Warns the hazard or danger
D] Gives information of safety provision
18] One micrometer (U] is equal to...
A] 0.1mm
B] 0.01mm
C] 0.001mm
D] 0.0001mm
19] The caliper meant for measuring the width of a slot is...
A] Odd leg caliper
B] Outside caliper
C] Jenny caliper
D] Inside calliper

Calliper

20] The size of the dividers are specified by the -----------
A] Total length of legs
B] Distance between the points when fully opened
C] Length of legs without points
D] distance between the pivot and the point
21] The instrument used to mark parallel lines, parallel to the datum edge is -
A] jenny caliper
B] Divider
C] Outside calliper
D] Inside calliper
22] Which one of the following is an indirect measuring tool?
A] Outside caliper
B] Vernier calliper
C] Steel rule

D] Outside micrometer

23] For cutting thin tubing, the most suitable pitch of the hacksaw blade is...

A] 1.8mm

B] 1.4mm

C] 1mm

D] <u>0.8mm</u>

24] For cutting solid brass, the most suitable pitch of the hacksaw blade is...

A] <u>1.8mm</u>

B] 1.4mm

C] 1mm

D] 0.8mm

Hacksaw frame

25] A new hacksaw blade after a few strokes becomes loose because of the...

A] <u>Stretching of the blade</u>

B] Wing-nut threads being worn out

C] Wrong pitch of the blade

D] Improper selection of the set of saws.

26] While cutting small diameter pipes, it is advisable to watch regularly and ensure that...

A] The cut is along the curved line

B] <u>More saw teeth are in contract</u>

C] The work is not overheated

D] Proper balancing of hacksaw is maintained

27] The vice clamps are used to...

A] Protect hard jaws

B] Clamp the work pieces rigidly

C] <u>Protect the finished surfaces</u>
D] Prevent the movable jaw being filed
28] The reference surface during marking is provided by the…
A] Surface gauge
B] Workpiece
C] Drawing of the work
D] <u>Marking table surface</u>
29] The size of an engineer's vice is specified by the…
A] Length of the movable jaw
B] <u>Width of the jaws</u>
C] Height of the vice
D] Maximum opening of the jaws
30] The part of the universal surface gauge which helps to draw a parallel line along a datum edge is the..
A] Rocker arm
B] Snug
C] Fine adjustment screw
D] <u>Guide pins</u>

Universal surface guage

31] Scribers are made of…
A] Mild steel
B] <u>High carbon steel</u>
C] Brass
D] Cast iron
32] Portion of the hammer used for fixing the handle is…
A] Face

B] Peen

C] Cheek

D] <u>Eye hole</u>

33] Weight of the hammer for the marking purpose is...

A] <u>250g</u>

B] 500g

C] 1 kg

D] 2 kgs

Hammer

34] The size of the dividers are specified by the...

A] Total length of the legs

B] Distance between the points when fully opened

C] Length of legs without the points

D] <u>Distance between the pivot and the point</u>

35] The included angle of the groove of 'V' block is always....

A] 45°

B] 60°

C] 90°

D] <u>120°</u>

36] 'V' blocks are available in grades of...

A] <u>A & B</u>

B] A,B & C

C] 1,2 & 3

D] 1 & 2

37] 'V' blocks of grade 'B' are made of

A] <u>Cast iron</u>

B] Mild steel

C] Steel

D] Cast steel

38] Name the punch used to locate the centre.

A] Prick punch 30°

B] Prick punch 60°

C] Centre punch

D] Dot punch

Centre punch

39] The point angle of centre punch is --------

A] 30°

B] 50°

c] 900

D] 1200

40] Punches are used for forming ---------of any shape

A] Holes

B] Mining

C] Knurling

D] Reaming

41] Generally the length of the handle of the vice is ----------

A] 1.5 times the normal size of the vice

B] 2.5 times the normal size of the vice

C] 3.5 times the normal size of the vice

D] 4.5 times the normal size of the vice

Bench vice

42] Bench vice spindle is made of ....
A] mild steel
B] Cast iron
C] Tool steel
D] Bronze

43] The convexity of files helps...
A] To file concave surfaces
B] To file convex surfaces
C] To prevent rounding of edges of work
D] The file to become straight when pressure is applied

Files

44] Which file used for filling wood, leather and other soft material? .
A] Single cut file
B] Double cut file
c] Rasp cut file
D] Curved cut file

45] File used is used for ------------
A] Cleaning the work piece

C] Renewing the file teeth
<u>B] cleaning the file teeth</u>
D] Cleaning the chips
46] File card is used to --------
A] Clean the work piece
C] Renew the file teeth
<u>B] Clean the file teeth</u>
47] The point angle of scriber is -----------
A] 30°
B] 60°
C] 5° to 10°
<u>D] 12° to 15°</u>
48] The cutting angle for chipping cast iron is...
A] 37.5∘
B] 55∘
C] <u>60∘</u>
D] 90∘

49] The chisel will dig into the material when...
A] The rake angle is more
B] The clearance angle is too low
C] <u>The angle of inclination is more</u>
D] The angle of inclination is too low
50] A slight convexity is given to the cutting edge to...
A] Cut curved surfaces
B] Cut sharp corners
C] <u>Prevent digging of the ends</u>
D] Allow the lubricant to enter
51] Surface plates are made of...
A] High grade cast steel
B] <u>Fine-grained cast iron</u>
C] Alloy steels

D] Wrought iron

52] Surface plates are specified by their length and breadth & are in
A] decimetre
B] Cubic meter
C] Cylindrical
53] Ribs are given on the unmachined portion of the angle plate for...
A] Easy handling
B] Convenience in manufacturing
C] Clamping while setting on machines
D] Rigidity and to prevent distortion
54] The slots on the angle plate are given for...
A] Reducing weight
B] Aligning the work
C] Lifting using hooks
D] Accommodating bolts.
55] The size of the angle plates is stated by...
A] Weight
B] Length
C] Length x width
D] Size number
Q 1) The first formed round dark portion of the tree is called ....
A) Ring
B) Pith
C) Bark
D) Cortex
Q 2) Which of the following can resist attack by white ants?
A) Deodar
B) Teak
C) Chir
D) Kail

Q 3) Which saw would be best choice for cutting an opening in wallboard for a switch box?

A) Key hole saw

B) Coping saw

C) Hacksaw

D) Back saw

Q 4) Name the part of the band saw machine which is provided between the wheels to support the work piece.

A) Table

B) Arm

C) Guide post

D) Column

Q 5) When a tree grows, many of its branches fall and the stump of these branches in the trunk is covered. In the

sawn pieces of timber the stump of fallen branches appear as ....

A) Spot

B) Knot

C) Ridge

D) Wedge

Q 6) In the figure given below, which one is dovetail joint?

A) Joint A

B) Joint B

C) Joint C

D) Joint D

Q 7) Identify what is shown in figure given below.

A) Pins

B) Ribs

C) Dowels

D) Keys

Q 8) Which of these joints is so weak that it has to be reinforced with steel plates or brackets when building roof

trusses?

A) Dovetail joint

B) Bridle joint

C) Butt joint

D) Mortise and tenon joint

Q 9) The distance from a given point on one thread to the corresponding point on the next thread is called ....

A) Helix
B) Lead
C) Pitch
D) Flat
Q 10) Which type of lock is NOT permanently attached to the door?
A) Pad lock
B) Knob lock
C) Deadbolt
D) Camlock
Q 11) A clicking noise on a band saw indicates ....
A) A broken wheel guard
B) A crack in the blade
C) Electrical power tripping
D) Nothing wrong
Q 12) What is the type of hinge shown in figure given below?
A) Butt hinge
B) Lift off hinge
C) Flush hinge
D) Security butt hinge
Q 13) The size of a tablesaw is determined by the ....
A) Height of the table
B) Shaft diameter
C) Blade diameter
D) Blade width
Q 14) The box shown in figure given below is called ....
A) Carpenter s box
B) Shaping box
C) Slitting box
D) Mitre box
Q 15) The tool used to test squareness of wood is ....
A) Ruler
B) Framing square
C) Try square
D) Combination square
Q 16) What is used to extract nails?
A) Ball pein hammer
B) Claw hammer
C) Mallet

D) Sledge hammer

Q 17) Figure below shows a piece of wood held in a vice. When using a plane, which direction should it move?

A) From left to right

B) From right to left

C) In any direction

D) Direction of movement is not important

Q 18) Which tool is used to make a fine cut in wooden workpiece?

A) Hand saw

B) Wooden saw

C) Tenon saw

D) Rip saw

Q 19) Which statement is NOT true with respect to the tool shown in figure below?

A) It is called brace

B) It is used with auger bits

C) It is used for drilling small diameter holes

D) It allows a lot of force to be applied to the drill bit

Q 20) Freshly cut lumber that has not been dried is called ....

A) Raw lumber

B) Fresh lumber

C) Green lumber

D) Base lumber

Q 21) The marks put on boards or pieces to keep them in order during gluing, joining and assembly, are called

....

A) Assembly marks

B) Witness marks

C) Visible marks

D) Limiting marks

Q 22) The post (figure given below) at the top or bottom of a stairway that supports the handrail, is called ....

A) Newel

B) Muntin

C) Ogee

D) Mould

Q 23) The angle at which the leading edge of the teeth are cut on a saw blade, is called

A) Face

B) Rake

C) Cutting angle

D) Clearance angle

Q 24) The kind of door used in fire exits is ....

A) Double action door

B) Panel door with panic bar

C) Panel door

D) Revolving door

Q 25) The disadvantage of sliding door is .... of cabinet opening is available.

A) One-half

B) One-third

C) One-fourth

D) One-fifth

Q 26) The upper most member of a door frame is called ....

A) Door head

B) Door roller

C) Door closer

D) Door jamb

Q 27) The member which is placed horizontally to support common rafter of a sloping roof, is ....

A) Purlin

B) Cleat

C) Batten

D) Strut

Q 28) Which of these is NOT a type of truss?

A) King post truss

B) Queen post truss

C) Prince post truss

D) Pratt truss

Q 29) The outer protective layer of a tree is called ....

A) Bark

B) Bast

C) Cambium

D) Sap wood

Q 30) The ratio of rise to span of a truss is called ....

A) Scale

B) Lead

C) Peak

D) Pitch

Q 31) A tool similar to an axe with the blade perpendicular to the handle, used to carve wood, is called ....

A) Awl

B) Adze

C) Scraper

D) Gouge

Q 32) When you use a chisel, it is important that you ....

A) Keep both hands behind all the times

B) Hit harder if chisel is blunt

C) Chisel across the grains if possible

D) Use the biggest possible chisel at all the times

Q 33) Which tool can produce mouldings, trim edges, form recesses and cut grooves?

A) Jack plane

B) Belt sander

C) Reciprocating saw

D) Router

Q 34) A jointer is a tool designed to ....

A) Cut mitres

B) Apply glue

C) Plane surfaces

D) Rip narrow stock

Q 35) It is a knife which has blade between two handles. The handles are at right angles to the blade. It is used to

smooth a surface by pulling the blade over the stock. Name the tool.

A) Pullknife

B) Drawknife

C) Right angle knife

D) Bridge knife

Q 36) A hxagonal wrench is also known as ....

A) Allen wrench

B) Stillson wrench

C) Socket wrench

D) Ratchet wrench

Q 37) Figure given below shows two types of ....

A) Casters
B) Cambers
C) Rollers
D) Drag wheels
Q 38) The preferable way to cut the ends of a number of boards at the same angle is to use ....
A) Mitre box
B) Protractor
C) Combination square
D) Combination bevel
Q 39) You have a short section of lumber which you want to round off. Name the suitable file for this work.
A) Single cut
B) Double cut
C) Curved cut
D) Rasp cut
Q 40) Black sandpaper used to smooth metal and take off rust is ....
A) Emery
B) Aluminium oxide
C) Silicon carbide
D) Pumice
Q 41) Which of these is NOT an abrasive mineral used in woodworking?
A) Garnet
B) Ceramic
C) Silicon carbide
D) Calcium carbide
Q 42) Before turning wood on a lathe, make sure it is ....
A) Hardwwood
B) Free of saw dust
C) Free of defects
D) Softwood
Q 43) What adjustment on wood turning lathe you should make before sanding or polishing?
A) Move the tool rest closer to the stock
B) Remove the tool rest
C) Add lighting to the work area
D) Add a second tool rest
Q 44) What can help prevent slips and falls on shop floor?

A) Using short ladders

B) Wearing leather soled shoes

C) Keeping the floor free of clutter and wiping up spills

D) Keeping an even layer of sawdust on the floor

Q 45) When the safety rules refer to horseplay ,

A) Fooling around

B) Throwing things around

C) Animals on shop floor

D) Playing game of horses

Q 46) When using a plane, make adjustments carefully because the blade is ....

A) Soft

B) Beakable

C) Sharp

D) Expensive

Q 47) A thin layer of expensive wood bonded to a thicker piece of cheaper plywood to give the appearance of the

expensive wood but at reduced price is called .....

A) Copse

B) Veneer

C) Thicket

D) Lumber

Q 48) A liquid preparation that dries to a hard lustrous coating is ....

A) Wax

B) Primer

C) Varnish

D) Sticker

Q 49) What is f in the wood turning lathe shown in figure given below?

A) Headstock

B) Lock knob

C) Tool post

D) Tailstock

Q 50) What type of surface is produced when facing operation is done on a lathe?

A) Flat

B) Taper

C) Cylindrical

D) Conical

Q 51) What might you use to hold together two pieces of wood if you are planning to glue them?

A) Hex tool

B) Biscuit joiner

C) C - clamp

D) Lever

Q 52) In CNC machines, the mode .... Is helpful when you are trying out a new program.

A) MDI

B) Single block

C) Edit

D) Initializing

Q 53) Plumb bob is used to verify the ....

A) Horizontal level

B) Vertical level

C) Parallel level

D) Surface level

Q 54) Which of the the following fire extinguisher is suitable for electrical fire?

A) Dry chemicals

B) Water

C) Foam

D) Soda acid

Q 55) Water is used to extinguish__________.

A) Class-A fires

B) Class-B fires

C) Class-C fires

D) All of these

Q 56) Which one of the following is not a type of straight cutting saw?

A) Bow saw

B) Rip saw

C) Tenon saw

D) Dovetail saw

Q 57) Which tool is used by carpenter sawing along the grains?

A) Plane

B) Chisel

C) Rip saw

D) Hammer

Q 58) Compared to other types of saws, tenon saws have______________.

A) More teeth per inch

B) Less teeth per inch

C) Same teeth per inch

D) None of these

Q 59) What is the use of circular saw ?

A) Ripping

B) Mitre cutting

C) Bevel cutting

D) All of these

Q 60) The length of the trying plane is___________.

A) 600-700 mm

B) 700-800 mm

C) 450-500 mm

D) 800-900 mm

Q 61) Which part indicate the age of a tree?

A) Pith

B) Ring

C) Bark

D) Cortex

Q 62) What is the scientific name of wood?

A) Xylem

B) Xylastrus orbiculatus

C) Parenchyma

D) Cycadophyta

Q 63) Which of the following is an example of soft wood?

A) Deodar

B) Sal

C) Oak

D) Mahogany

Q 64) The cracking on the outside of a log due to shrinkage of exterior surface is called________________.

A) Wind crack

B) Ring shake

C) Upset

D) Wane

Q 65) Which of the following is not a type of Chisel ?

A) Hot chisels

B) Bench chisels

C) Butt chiselz

D) Cabinet chisels

Q 66) The quality of timber does not depend upon_______________.

A) Size of tree

B) Maturity of tree

C) Weight of timber

D) Type of tree

Q 67) Identify the hand tool shown in the figure?

A) Gimlet

B) Screwdriver

C) Star-head Screwdriver

D) Flat nose plier

Q 68) Identify the hand tool shown in the figure?

A) Hand drill

B) Gimlet

C) Ratchet brace

D) Electric drill

Q 69) The_______________ joint is used in high quality furniture drawer construction.

A) Lapped dovetail

B) Rabbit

C) Dado

D) Lap

Q 70) which one of the following is a box joint?

A) Comb joint

B) Tee halving

C) Corner halving

D) Tenon and mortise

Q 71) _______________ joints are employed to extend the length of a member by joining two pieces of timber.

A) Lengthening

B) Angle

C) Lapped

D) Widening

Q 72) Density is calculated by_______.

A) Mass ÷ Volume

B) Volume ÷ Mass

C) Volume X Mass

D) Weight X Thickness

Q 73) Which of the following is a part of screw driver?

A) Blade

B) Tip

C) Shank

D) All of these

Q 74) Identify the hand tool shown in the figure?

A) Pincer

B) Combination plier

C) Tong

D) Flat nose plier

Q 75) Which conversion method is shown in figure given below?

A) Tangential sawing

B) Parallel sawing

C) Radial sawing

D) Quarter sawing

Q 76) Fiber board are also known as __________________.

A) Pressed wood

B) Passed wood

C) Light wood

D) None of these

Q 77) A thin sheet of wood rotary cut, sliced or sawn from a log used as a superior facing to inferior wood to form

plywood is_____________.

A) Veneer

B) Particle sheet

C) Cross bond layer

D) Vinyl sheet

Q 78) It is made by bonding together thin layers of wood in a way that the grains of each layer are at right angles

of the adjacent layer. It is_____________.

A) Plywood

B) Building wood

C) Cork board

D) Hard board

Q 79) Which layer is called "core" in plywood?

A) Middle layer

B) Upper layer

C) Top layer

D) Side layer

Q 80) Which one of the statement is not an advantage of plywood?

A) It will shrink and warp easily

B) It is manufactured in very large size

C) It is lighter in weight

D) It can be easily worked and bent in shaped and designs

Q 81) Which part of the tree is mostly useful for carpentry work?

A) Heart wood

B) Sap wood

C) Bark

D) Root

Q 82) Which vice is used for sharpening the saw ?

A) saw vice

B) carpenter vice

C) Bar clamp

D) C- clamp

Q 83) Which of the following is not a preservative of timber?

A) Glue

B) Tar

C) Creosote

D) Chemical salt

Q 84) The angle of single cut file is__________.

A) $60°$

B) $51°$

C) $70°$

D) $90°$

Q 85) A file used to make saw pointed is__________.

A) Triangular file

B) Half round file

C) Irregular file

D) Auger bit file

Q 86) "Knot" is a kind of defect in timber, which happens due to __________.

A) Natural cause

B) Seasoning

C) Attack by fungi

D) Attack by insects

Q 87) Which is the most rapid and effective method of seasoning?

A) Electric seasoning

B) Kiln seasoning

C) Natural seasoning

D) Chemical seasoning

Q 88) Which of the following is a type of non-refractory timber?

A) Deoder

B) Teak

C) Sheesham

D) Sal

Q 89) _________________ joint is the simplest form of carpentry joint.

A) Dovetail

B) Rabbit

C) Finger

D) Lap

Q 90) What type of wood is best for furniture?

A) Cherry

B) White Oak

C) Pine

D) Teak

Q 91) Identify the chair shown in the figure.

A) Wood armed chair

B) Steel armed chair

C) Wood armless chair

D) Wood stool

Q 92) Which of the following is a type of circular saw blade?

A) Crosscut

B) Ripping

C) Combination

D) All of these

Q 93) Which one of the sawing operation is not related to circular saw machine?

A) Rip saw

B) Mould cutting

C) Miter cutting

D) Cross cutting

Q 94) Before planing, we must inspect the surface for_____________.

A) Turning

B) Warping

C) Correct dimensions

D) Trimming

Q 95) The maximum tiling angle of the band saw machine is_______.

A) 45°

B) 60°

C) 90°

D) 120°

Q 96) Band saw sizes are determined by the____________.

A) Wheel diameter

B) Blade thickness

C) Table size

D) None of these

Q 97) Hollow chisel mortising machine combines the cuting of a ____________ chisel with the action of the drill

bit in the centre.

A) Four-sided

B) Two-sided

C) Three-sided

D) None of these

Q 98) Mortiser machine is a ____________ machine, which is used to drill square and rectangular in

timber.

A) Wood working

B) Metal working

C) Clay working

D) None of these

Q 99) What is the name of carpenter tool shown in the figure?

A) Claw Hammer

B) Ball peen Hammer

C) Cross peenHammer

D) Straight peen Hammer

Q 100) Which of the following is not a type of furniture table?

A) Tea table

B) Computer table

C) Dining table

D) Excel table

Q 101) The power plane is essentially a ______________that drives a cutter bar.

A) high-speed motor

B) high-speed engine

C) Low-speed motor

D) None of these

Q 102) Sanding discs are installed using ____________.

A) Two wrenches of different sizes

B) Pressure-sensitive adhesive

C) Tension knob

D) Chuck key

Q 103) Identify the type of sanding machine shown in the figure.

A) Disc sander

B) Belt sander

C) Spindle sander

D) Gear sander

Q 104) In frame and panel construction, the outside vertical frame members is______.

A) Stiles

B) Rails

C) Lock rails

D) Mullion

Q 105) _________ windows are similar to the sliding doors and the shutter moves on the roller bearings, either

horizontally or vertically.

A) Sliding

B) Swinging

C) Rolling

D) Metal

Q 106) Sliding window is a type of window in which shutter moves__________.

A) Horizontally

B) Vertically

C) Either Horizontally or Vertically

D) None of these

Q 107) What is the main purpose of putty on a surface?

A) To fill any hairline cracks or holes on the surface of the wall

B) To create a uniform, levelled out surface ready for painting,

C) To prevent or reduce water seepage

D) All of these

Q 108) Name the accessory which is NOT used in drilling machine.

A) Tool holder

B) Sleeve

C) Socket

D) Drill chuck

Q 109) A _______________ is a power tool that can perform heavy-duty tasks such as drilling and chiseling hard

materials.

A) Rotary hammer

B) Jack plane

C) Belt sander

D) Reciprocating saw

Q 110) A wooden piece provided at the Ridge line of a sloping roof is known as the _______________.

A) Rafter

B) Ridge

C) Gable

D) Pitch

Q 111) In ____________ roofs, the common Rafter are provided to itself without any intermediate support.

A) Single

B) Double

C) Purlin

D) Trussed

Q 112) Figure given below shows a_______________.

A) Queen post truss

B) King post truss

C) Both queen post and king post truss

D) None of these

Q 113) _______________ floors consists of single joist which are placed below the floor boards.

A) Single joint timber floor

B) Single joist timber floor

C) Single timber floor

D) Joist Floor

Q 114) The______________size determines the coarseness of a sheet of sand paper.

A) Grit

B) Sand

C) Paper

D) Aluminium oxide

Q 115) Which tool is used by a carpenter for smoothing wood?

A) Plane

B) Chisel

C) Rip saw

D) Rasp

Q 116) Changes in wood moisture content can result in ______________________of wood which can stress and crack coatings.

A) Swelling

B) Shrinkage

C) Swelling and shrinkage both

D) None of these

Q 117) ________________ is particularly effective at removing iron stains from wood.

A) Oxalic acid

B) Bleach

C) Water

D) Oil

Q 118) Primers are used____________.

A) Before painting

B) After painting

C) Together with paint

D) None of these

Q 119) The most durable varnish is_____________.

A) Oil varnish

B) Water varnish

C) Sprit varnish

D) All of these

Q 120) In Wood working CNC Router, CNC stands for __________________ .

A) Computer Numeric Control

B) Control Numeric Control

C) Computer Number Control

D) Counter Numeric Control

Q 121) In CNC operation G00 is a code for_______________.

A) Rapid positioning

B) Linear interpolation

C) Circular interpolation

D) None of these

Q 122) In CNC operation M00 is a code for_______________.

A) Program stop

B) Spindle start

C) Tool change

D) Coolant on

Q 123) What should be the moisture content when the density of timber is determined?

A) 12%

B) 18%

C) 20%

D) 22%

Q 124) The main component of wood turning lathe machine is___________.

A) Head stock and spindle

B) Tail stock and poppet barrel

C) Bed and tool rest

D) All of these

Q 125) Spindle turning involves turning stock held between the live center and the ____________.

A) Spur

B) tool rest

C) Headstock

D) Dead center

Q 126) The FIRST priority when working at a machine is-

A) Don t make any mistakes

B) Watch the other people around

C) Always thinking about safety

D) None of these

Q 127) Wax polish on wood comes under in which of the following category?

A) Evaporative

B) Clear

C) Water based

D) None of these

Answer Key

Question No.	Option	Question No.	Option	Question No.	Option	Question No.	Option	Question No.	Option
1	B	31	B	61	B	91	A	121	A
2	B	32	A	62	A	92	D	122	A
3	A	33	D	63	A	93	B	123	A
4	A	34	C	64	A	94	C	124	D
5	B	35	B	65	A	95	A	125	D
6	D	36	A	66	A	96	A	126	A
7	C	37	A	67	A	97	A	127	A
8	C	38	A	68	A	98	A		
9	C	39	D	69	A	99	A		
10	A	40	A	70	A	100	D		
11	B	41	D	71	A	101	A		
12	B	42	C	72	A	102	C		
13	C	43	B	73	D	103	A		
14	D	44	C	74	A	104	A		
15	C	45	A	75	D	105	A		
16	B	46	C	76	A	106	A		

17	A	47	B	77	A	107	D
18	C	48	C	78	A	108	A
19	C	49	D	79	A	109	A
20	C	50	A	80	A	110	B
21	B	51	C	81	A	111	A
22	A	52	B	82	A	112	A
23	B	53	B	83	A	113	B
24	B	54	A	84	A	114	A
25	A	55	A	85	A	115	A
26	A	56	A	86	A	116	C
27	A	57	C	87	A	117	A
28	C	58	A	88	A	118	A
29	A	59	D	89	D	119	A
30	D	60	A	90	D	120	A

Enter Caption

58] One of the functions of flux in gas welding is...

A] dissolve the metal oxides

B] reduce the melting point of mental

C] increase the flame temperature

D] increase the root penetration

59] The angle of vee groove of a single vee but joint for cast iron welding is...

A] 60°

B] 70°

C] 80°

D] 90°

60] On which of the following factors, the choice of flux for gas welding depend?

A] type of material to be joined

B] type of edge penetration

C] type of fuel gas

D] type of flame used

61].What is the nozzle size required to bronze weld 10mm thick cast iron job?

A] 5

B] 7

C] <u>10</u>

D] 13

bronze welding

62] State the suitable filler rod for bronze welding of cast iron

A] brass

B] <u>silicon bronze</u>

C] manganese bronze

D] super silicon cast iron

63] In bronze welding of cast iron, the base metal is heated upto a temperature of...

A] 300∘C

B] <u>650∘C</u>

C] 1000◦C

D] 1300◦C

64] Name the filler rod used for fusion welding of copper

A] manganese bronze rod

B] copper silver alloy rod

C] silicon bronze rod

D] pure copper rod

65] The divergence allowance required for gas welding a 300mm long copper butt joint is...

A] 1 to 2 mm

B] 2 to 3 mm

C] 3 to 4 mm

D] 4 to 5 mm

66] The type of edge preparation done for gas welding a 4mm thick copper butt joint is...

A] single bevel

B] single V

C] double V

D] square

67] The nozzle size used for bronze welding of a 3.15 mm thick copper butt joint is...

A] 5

B] 7

C] 10

D] 13

68] State the filler rod size required for welding a butt joint on 3mm thick brass sheet

A] 1.6 mm

B] 2 mm

C] 2.5 mm

D] 3 mm

69] Name the weld defect which will occur if a No] 3 nozzle is used for welding a 3 mm thick brass sheet

A] undercut

B] burn through

C] porosity

D] lack of penetration

<u>aluminium butt joint</u>

70] The size of nozzle used to gas weld 3.15 mm thick aluminium butt joint is...

A] 13

B] 10

C] 7

D] <u>5</u>

71] Nozzle size used for welding a 2 mm thick stainless steel sheet as a butt joint is...

A] 2

B] 3

C] 5

D] 7

72] What is the value of preheating temperature for gas welding of aluminium?

A] 100 to 120∘C

B] <u>150 to 180∘C</u>

C] 180 to 200∘C

D] 210 to 250∘C

Q 5] The source of heat in gas welding is ________

A] voltage

B] thermit

C] <u>gas flame</u>

D] Electricity

Q 6] Which of the following equipment is used in arc welding ?

A] <u>Electrode holder</u>

B] Oxygen gas cylinder

C] Welding blowpipe

D] None of these

Q 7] Which of the following equipment is used in gas welding ?
A] Gas regulator
B] Oxygen gas cylinder
C] Welding blowpipe
D] All of these
Q 8] Which of the following is a metal joining process?
A] Welding
B] Brazing
C] Riveting
D] All of these
Q 9] Which of the following method makes a permanent joint?
A] Welding
B] Riveting
C] Bolting
D] None of these
Q 10] Identify the given equipment]
A] Tip cleaner
B] Welding screen
C] Electrode holder
D] None of these
Q 11] Which of the following statement is true about neutral flame?\
A] Complete combustion takes place in this flame]
B] For welding mild steel neutral flame is used]
C] There are two zones in neutral flame]
D] All of these
Q 12] Which gas is produced when reacting with calcium carbide water?
A] Acetylene
B] Oxygen
C] Nitrogen
D] Argon
Q 13] Which type of oxy-acetylene flame is used for welding mild steel?
A] Neutral flame
B] Oxidising flame
C] Carburising flame
D] Acidic flame
Q 14] Which of the following is not a type of oxy-acetylene flame
A] Neutral flame
B] Oxidising flame

C] Carburising flame

D] <u>Acidic flame</u>

Q 15] What is the chemical formula of acetylene gas?

A] CH

B] CH2

C] <u>C2H2</u>

D] None of these

Q 16] Identify the type of oxy-acetylene gas flame shown in the picture]

A] Neutral flame

B] Oxidising flame

C] <u>Carburising flame</u>

D] None of these

Q 17] Oxygen is approximately _____% in the atmosphere]

A] 78

B] 0]03

C] <u>21</u>

D] 7

Q 18] What is the chemical symbol of oxygen gas?

A] C

B] CH

C] N2

D] <u>O2</u>

Q 19] The color of the oxygen gas cylinder is _____]

A] green

B] <u>black</u>

C] red

D] Blue

Q 20] The work of gas regulator is _____]

A] getting different types of flames

B] mixing the mixture of gases into the expected proportion

C] to clean hose pipe

D] <u>setting up the working pressure</u>

Q 21] Nozzle of gas welding blowpipe is made up of which metal?

A] Mild steel

B] <u>Copper</u>

C] Cast iron

D] Tin

Q 22] Identify the equipment shown in the picture]

A] Gas regulator

B] <u>Welding blowpipe</u>

C] Tip cleaner

D] Spark lighter

Q 23] Which of the following is used as a flux in brazing?

A] Borax

B] Boric acid

C] <u>Both borax and boric acid</u>

D] None of these

Q 24] Which of the following flame is suitable for preheating before flame

cutting?

A] Oxidizing flame

B] <u>Neutral flame</u>

C] Carburizing flame

D] none of these

Q 25] What happens if a very little oxygen is supplied in gas cutting?

A] The metal will be cooled down

B] The kerf will be narrow

C] The kerf will be wide

D] <u>The metal will not cut completely</u>

Q 26] Which of the following is a type of manifold system?

A] Portable

B] Stationary

C] <u>Both portable and stationary</u>

D] None of these

Q 27] Identify the welding defect shown in the picture]

A] Overlap

B] <u>Undercut</u>

C] Crack\दरार

D] Lack of fusion

Q 28] Name the gas welding defect in which number of pinholes formed on the surface of deposited metal]

A] Crack

B] <u>Porosity</u>

C] Lack of fusion

D] check and forget method

Q 29] Which of the following equipment is used in oxy-acetylene gas cutting?

A] Spark lighter

B] Tip cleaner

C] Cutting torch

D] <u>All of these</u>

Q 30] Which of the following metal can be cut by oxy acetylene gas cutting process?

A] <u>Mild steel</u>

B] Aluminium

C] Copper

D] All of these

Plumber Theory Level-1

Q 1. Identify the plumbing symbol shown below.

A). Ball valve

B). Relief valve

C). Check valve

D). Power valve

Q 2. A bit brace is used to ____________.

A). Bore a hole

B). Ream a hole

C). Thread a hole

D). Grind a hole

Q 3. The tool shown in figure given below is called____________.

A) Pipe wrench

B) Stillson wrench

C) Both pipe wrench and stillson wrench

D) Neither pipe wrench nor stillson wrench

Q 4. A soldering bit consists of a piece of __________ fastened to an iron rod with a wooden handle.

A). Tin

B). Copper

C). Lead

D). Zinc

Q 5. There are many basic forms that can be applied to the end of a tube. Which form is applied by using the tool shown in figure given below?

A) Reduction

B) Expansion

C) Flaring

D) Beading

Q 6. What causes clogging of sewers?

A). Silting

B). Low discharge

C). Domestic waste thrown in manhole

D). All of these

Q 7. Figure given below shows a:-

A) Floor trap

B) Gully trap,

C) Bottle trap

D) Intercepting trap

Q 8. In a single stack waste system ____________.

A). Soil waste is discharged separate to waste water

B). All waste is discharged to a single waste pipe

C). Only waste water is discharged

D). Only soil waste is discharged

Q 9. What degree of pressure is required to ensure smooth drainage?

A). Low pressure

B). High pressure

C). It is not a matter of pressure

D). It is a matter of gravity

Q 10. A device installed in a drainage system to prevent reverse flow is ____________.

A). Back flow valve

B). Back-siphonage

C). Backflow preventer

D). Back-vent pipe

Q 11. What is a bidet?

A). A sanitary appliance to wash excretory organs

B). A kind of trap

C). A kind of mixing tap

D). A type of urinal

Q 12. There are different types of water reservoir tanks in use. What is NOT true about G.I. tanks? A). It is generally rectangular or square in shape

B). It lasts long

C). It is subject to corrosion

D). Its maintenance cost is high

Q 13. A tub surrounded by three walls of tile is an example of which type of tub?

A) Enclosed

B) Walk-in

C) Whirlpool

D) Free standing

Q 14. A basin supported by a free standing base (figure below) is called:-

A) Wall hung basin

B) Above counter basin

C) Pedestal basin

D) Inset basi

Q 15. What is NOT true about "Waterless Urinal"?

A). It does not have a pipe for water intake

B). Gravity drains the urinal

C). Outflow pipe is connected to the regular flushing system

D). It is flushed

Q 16. A tap is also called a _______________.

A). Facet

B). Fuller

C). Faucet

D). Faller

Q 17. To prevent flow in wrong direction, valve of the type shown in figure is used. What is this valve called?

A). Seat valve

B). Butterfly valve

C). Check valve

D). Globe valve

Q 18. Which of these can cause leakage in pipes?

A) Rusting of pipes in advanced stage

B) Degraded seals

C) Excess water pressure

D) All of these

Q 19. Which type of sewer serves as an outlet for large territory?

A). Lateral sewer

B). Main sewer

C). Branch sewer

D). Separate sewer

Q 20. Which of these is known as shut off valve?

A). Air relief valve

B). Sluice valve

C). Pressure relief valve

D). Altitude valve

Q 21. Watercolumn that seals the escape of unhealthy gases in sanitary drainage system is: -

A). Siphon level

B). Water seal

C). Air lock

D). Air chamber

Q 22. A type of vent installed to ventilate soil and waste pipe and connecting branches is:-

A). Loop vent

B). Relief vent

C). Unit vent

D). Circuit vent

Q 23. In a mixing tap, hot water connection is given to the ___________.

A). Right side of the user

B). Left side of the user

C). Either side of the user

D). Neither side of the user

Q 24. A seepage is defined as a sewage terminal ___________.

A). Receiving both liquid and solid waste

B). Receiving only liquid waste

C). Receiving only solid waste

D). Receiving direct human excrement

Q 25. What is being used in figure given below to clear blocked drain?

A). Sink piston

B). Sink plunger

C). Sink throat

D). Sink pusher

Q 26. After laying a sewer, a number of tests are done. In one test a ball is rolled down from upsteam side. This test is called ___________.

A). Water test

B). Air test

C). Test for obstruction

D). Smoke test

Q 27. The volume of liquid passing through a cross-section of a stream in unit time is called:-

A). Steady flow

B). Uniform flow

C). Continuous flow

D). Discharge

Q 28. A pipe fitting usually short with inside threads used to connect pipes with outside threaded ends is called:-

A). Nipple

B). Coupling

C). Union

D). Cross pipe

Q 29. What is the type of hydrant shown in figure given below?

A). Flush hydrant

B). Barrel hydrnt

C). Post hydrant

D). Plug hydrant

Q 30. The symbol shown below is of _______________.

A). Relief valve

B). Needle valve

C). Butterfly valve

D). Gate valve

Q 31. If your clothing catches fire, it is important to __________.

A). Run from the flames

B). Look for a fire extinguisher

C). Stop, drop and roll

D). Wait for help

Q 32. Dual system of water supply means:-

A). Continuous supply system

B). Pumping and intermittent system

C). Gravity and pumping system

D). Gravity and continuous supply system

Q 33. An electrochemical process in which one metal corrodes preferentially when it is electrical contact with another, in presence of an electrolyte, is called:-

A). Electrolytical corrosion

B). Electrical corrosion

C). Galvanic corrosion

D). Chemical corrosion

Q 34. ___________gloves are used to protect hands against contact with used soil, waste systems and sanitary appliances.

A). Rubber

B). General Purpose

C). Specialist

D). Woolen

Q 35. The following safety sign is used for_______________.

A). emergency phone

B). danger of high voltage

C). first aid station

D). emergency exit

Q 36. Scriber is ____________tool.

A). marking

B). measuring

C). planning

D) drilling

Q 37. Identify the following type of spanner:

A). Adjustable spanner

B). Double open-ended spanner

C). Ring spanner

D). Double ended ring spanner

Q 38. In an exogenous tree, the central rings surrounding the pith are called____________.

A). heart wood

B). cambium layer

C). cortex

D) annual rings

Q 39. Which of these timber defects is due to excessive compression in the tree when it was young?

A). upsets

B). wind cracks

C). shakes

D). knots

Q40. Fretsaw is used for cutting_______________.

A). sharp and fine curves

B). small holes in wood

C). straight surfaces

D) uneven surfaces

Q 41. The inner cone in neutral flame of welding is ___________in colour.

A). light blue

B). light green

C). red

D) brown

Q 42. In a welding blowpipe, which of these regulates the flow of incoming gases?

A). valves

B). mixing chamber

C). body

D). tip

Q 43. Soft solders are usually alloys of_______________.

A). lead and tin

B). copper and iron

C). copper and aluminium

D). iron and zinc

Q 44. In___________brazing, the assembled parts are dipped in a flux bath kept at a temperature required to melt the filler metal.

A). dip

B). furnace

C). torch

D) electric

Q 45. _______________is a tool used in masonry to smooth noticeable joints in a facing.

A). Joint filler

B). Hawk

C). Square Trowel

D). Shovel

Q 46. In___________position, a brick is laid flat with the short end of the brick exposed.

A). Header

B). Soldier

C). Sailor

D) Shiner

Q 47. In a ratchet brace,_______________spins around the frame as the brace is turned.

A). Sweep Handle

B). Header

C). Chuck

D) Ball bearing cup

Q 48. Identify the following type of valve:

A). Relief valve

B). Power valve

C). Ball valve

D) Mixing valve

Q 49. Which of these classes of GI pipes is the thinnest?

A). Class A

B). Class B

C). Class C

D) Class D

Q 50. Which of the following is not an advantage of GI pipes?

A). Mineral buildup

B). Fast assembly

C). Long life

D) Toughness

Q 51. HDPE pipes can carry: 2). chemicals 3). power cables 4). water 5). compressed gases Select the correct answer from the codes given below.

A). 1,2,3,4,5

B). 1,2,3

C). 4,5

D) 1,3,5

Q 52. ___________is used to combine or split a fluid flow.

A). Tee

B). Reducer

C). Union

D). Coupling

Q 53. Identify the given figure:

A). Reducer Union

B). Female Tee

C). Female Union

D). Flange

Q 54. Which of these covers the end of a pipe?

A). Plug

B). Nipple

C). Elbow

D). Tee

Q 55. Which of these is a suspended impurity found in water?

A). Clay

B). Organic salts

C). Amino acids

D). Bacteria

Q 56. Water hammer is also known as______________.

A). hydraulic shock

B). plumber's force

C). water logging

D). water freezing

Q 57. ______________pressure is the difference of atmospheric pressure and absolute pressure.

A). Gauge

B). Static

C). Differential

D). Vaccum

Q 58. Which of these sands is used for plastering work?

A). Fine sand

B). Coarse sand

C). Gravel sand

D). Mud sand

Q 59. __________is a formation of membrane designed to prevent water from entering or escaping c oncrete.

A). Waterproofing

B). Plastering

C). Manhole

D) Slaking

Q 60. Waste water from kitchen and bathroom is piped to a __________before emptying into a sewer.

A). gully trap

B). septic tank

C). manhole

D). dispersion trench

Q 61. Soak pit, dispersion trench, leaching cesspool etc.are used with______________.

A). Septic tank

B). Manhole

C). Concreting systems

D). Scaffolds

Q 62. ______________is the most common method for joining copper pipes.

A). Brazing

B). Soldering

C). Welding

D). Riveting

Q 63. For pipe laying, the trench width should be such as to provide a space of ______on either sides of a pipe.

A). 300 mm

B). 150 mm

C). 600 mm

D) 750 mm

Q 64. ______________are also referred as Overhead Tanks.

A). Elevated Storage Reservoirs

B). HDPE tanks

C). GI tanks

D). RCC tanks

Q 65. A suction pressure of 500 N/m^2 will reduce the water level in a basin by________.

A) 25 mm

B) 100 mm

C) 10 mm

D) 5 mm

Q 66. In a drainage system, foul gases escape into atmosphere by______________.

A) vent pipe

B) waste pipe

C) cesspool

D) anti-siphonage pipe

Q 67. The given figure depicts a__________trap.\ गि हुई आकृत ____________ ट्रैप को शिाजती है|

A) Q

B) P

C) R

D) S

Q 68. The area beneath the garden which contains pipes is called a
______________.

A) leaching field

B) playground

C) cesspool

D) waste pipe

Q 69. In order to clear bottle trap, ______________________________to gain access to the pipe.

A) base cap should be removed

B) base cap should be hammered

C) base cap should be broken

D) all fittings should be hammered

Q 70. What should be the ideal distance between water line and sewer line?

A) more than 3 metres

B) 1.5 metres

C) '0.5 metres

D) 'more than 5 metres

Q 71. Which of these is NOT a component of Rainwater Harvesting?

A) Soak pit

B) Catchment area

C) Conveyance system

D) Collection devices

Q 72. ______________are used to transfer the rainwater collected on the rooftops to the storage tanks.

A) Conveyance system

B) Open containers

C) Closed containers

D) Catchment area

Q 73. The limitation of rainwater harvesting is______________.

A) uncertainity of rainfall

B) use of open containers

C) automation of down-pipe flap

D) availability of collection devices

Q 74. In rainwater harvesting, down-pipe flap is used to______________.

A) selectively collect clean water for storage tanks

B) prevent algae growth in storage tank

C) provide a better catchment area

D) prevent breeding of mosquitoes in storage tank

Q 75. A pump moves the fluid by___________action.

A) mechanical

B) electrical

C) chemical

D) magnetic

Q 76. The backflow of water in a reciprocating displacement pump is prevented by means of_____________.

A) valve

B) piston rod

C) force rod

D) sealing

Q 77. Which of the following imparts energy to a fluid through centrifugal force in a centrifugal pump?

A) Rotary vanes

B) Casing

C) Bearings

D) Volute

Q 78. __________is used to draw more water from deep well than any other type of pump.

A) Air-lift pump

B) Booster pump

C) Mono-block pump

D) Rotary pump

Q 79. _____________is a valve where full flow is through a hole in a tapered plug.

A) Plug cock

B) Needle valve

C) Scour valve

D) Drain valve

Q 80. The building drain ventilating pipe should not be less than _____________in diameter.

A) 75 mm

B) 100 mm

C) 20 mm

D) 5 mm

Q 81. In a building, Q-trap is not used in _____________.

A) ground floor

B) first floor

C) second floor

D) third floor

Q 82. _________________is a simple collection point for waste water from a building.

A) Cesspool

B) Trap

C) Vent pipe

D) Hopper

Q 83. Specific Heat Capacity is highest in the case of_____________.

A) water

B) zinc

C) oil

D) steel

Q 84. The intensity of heat in a non-pressure type water heater is regulated by regulating the____________.

A) 'stop valve at inlet

B) outlet temperature

C) inlet temperature

D) 'supply

Q 85. Which of the following sets the temperature to a certain value so that the water is not heated above that value?

A) Thermostat

B) Thermocouple

C) Thermometer

D) Radiator

Q 86. Which of these saves energy by switching off the geyser and protect it from burning out?

A) Auto cut

B) Safety valve

C) Thermostat

D) Fusible plug

Q 87. With reference to solar water heating, ETC stands for____________.

A) Evacuated Tube Collectors

B) Estimated Time Collectors

C) Exact Time Collectors

D) Extra Tube Collectors

Q 88. In solar heating system, which of the following is used for small tanks?

A) Mild steel

B) Copper

C) Cast iron

D) Zinc

Q 89. Which of these is not used in manufacturing of AC pipes?

A) clay

B) silica

C) portland cement

D) asbestos fibre

Q 91. ______________ joint is also known as universal joint.

A) Flexible

B) Collar

C) Grooved

D) Union

Q 92. Mirror Test and Ball Test are carried out to check the______________.

A) alignment of pipes

B) accuracy of pipe joints

C) pipe bending

D) smoothness of inner surface of pipes

Q 93. Which of the following is a reason for water flowing around the stuffing box screw?

A) Gland nut is loose

B) Stuffing box packing is dry

C) Spindle is bent

D) Spindle thread is badly worn out

Q 94. The given plumbing symbol depicts______________.

A) Cold water

B) Vent line

C) Gas pipe

D) Hot water

Q 95. During execution, the mouth of pipes should be covered with empty gunny bags to avoid______________.

A) blockage

B) leakage

C) foul smell

D) mosquitoes

Level 1 Answer Key

Level 1 Answer Key

Question No.	Option
1	B
2	A
3	C
4	B
5	C
6	D
7	B
8	B
9	D
10	A
11	A
12	B
13	A
14	C
15	D
16	C
17	C
18	D
19	B

Question No.	Option
46	A
47	A
48	A
49	A
50	A
51	A
52	A
53	A
54	A
55	A
56	A
57	A
58	A
59	A
60	A
61	A
62	A
63	A
64	A

Question No.	Option
91	A
92	A
93	A
94	A
95	A

20	B		65	A
21	B		66	A
22	B		67	A
23	B		68	A
24	B		69	A
25	B		70	A
26	C		71	A
27	D		72	A
28	B		73	A
29	C		74	A
30	A		75	A
31	C		76	A
32	C		77	A
33	C		78	A
34	A		79	A
35	A		80	A
36	A		81	A
37	A		82	A
38	A		83	A
39	A		84	A
40	A		85	A
41	A		86	A
42	A		87	A
43	A		88	A
44	A		89	A
45	A		90	A

Plumber Theory Level-2

Q 1. It is a short stub of pipe having external male pipe threads at each end and used to connect two other fittings. It is called _____________.

A) Plug

B) Nipple,

C) Cap

D) Union

Q 2. In the figure given below, item '3' is called _____________.

A) ELL

B) TEE

C) Reducer

D) Elbow

Q 3. Which statement is NOT true about PVC pipes?

A). It is light in weight

B). It is corrosion free

C). It is cheaper than CI pipes

D). It can be used to carry hot water

Q 4. GI pipes are steel pipes with protective coating of _________.

A). Lead

B). Zinc

C). Tin

D). Antimony

Q 5. Acetylene gas is produced by reaction of water with ___________.

A). Calcium chloride

B). Calcium carbide

C). Calcium carbonate

D). Calcium bicarbonate

Q 6. Dissolved acetylene is stored in cylinders containing ___________.

A). Kerosene

B). Soluble oil

C). Acetone

D). Mineral oil

Q 7. Welding can be done in four positions as shown below. Name these positions in correct order from left to right.

A) Horizontal; Flat; Vertical; Overhead

B) Flat; Horizontal; Vertical; Overhead

C) Flat; Horizontal; Overhead; Vertical

D) Horizontal; Vertical; Overhead; Flat

Q 8. The most common solder is a combination of tin and lead. Which tin/lead combination has the lowest melting point?

A) 40% tin/60% lead

B) 50% tin / 50% lead

C) 60% tin / 40% lead

D) 63% tin / 37% lead

Q 9. What is the type of bond shown in figure given below?

A). Stretcher bond

B). English bond

C). Flemish bond

D). Soldier bond

Q 10. The size of a brick is __________.

A). 228 × 107 × 69 mm

B). 228 × 117 × 69 mm

C). 238 × 107 × 69 mm

D). 228 × 107 × 79 mm

Q 11. Shown in figure below is a tool used by a mason. It is called __________.

A) Trowel

B) Mortar pan

C) Hawk

D) Filler

Q 12. What is NOT true about bell-type cistern?

A). It is operated by a chain

B). Siphonic action is created in this system

C). It is very quiet system

D). When the chain is pulled, a bell is lifted

Q 13. The guidelines for preparation of mortar are given in__________.

A). IS 4455

B). IS 2250 - 1981

C). IS 3350 - 1981

D). IS 5567

Q 14. What is added to make mortar fire-proof?

A). Gypsum

B). Asbestos cement

C). Powdered glass

D). Aluminous cement

Q 15. What of these should be avoided in brick masonry?

A). Horizontal joints

B). Queen closer

C). Brick bat

D). Vertical joints

Q 16. Identify the bond shown in figure given below.

A) Soldier bond

B) Herringbone bond

C) Single Flemish Bond

D) Double Flemish Bond

Q 17. Identify what is shown in figure given below.

A) Queen closer

B) Bevelled closer

C) Mitred closer

D) King closer

Q 18. PVC plug is used to ______________.

A). Connect pipes of varying diameters

B). Connect two pipe lines

C). Seal pipes of small diameter

D). Seal ends of pipe line

Q 19. Which pipe fitting allows contents of two pipes to flow together into one pipe?

A). Lateral

B). Cross

C). Elbow

D). Return bend

Q 20. The choice of method for tube bending depends upon __________.

A). Diameter of tube

B). Wall thickness of tube

C). Minimum bend radius required

D). All of these

Q 21. What is the method of tube bending shown in figure given below?

A) Rotary draw bending

B) Ram bending

C) Compression bending

D) Roll bending

Q 22. Which of these statements is NOT true?

A). Manholes are provided in sewer pipes at suitable intervals

B).. Catch basins are generally provided in sewers for carrying drainage discharge

C). Inlets are generally provided in all sewers

D). None of these

Q 23. The asbestos cement pipes are generally laid ____________.

A). Horizontally

B). Vertically

C). At an angle of 30 degrees

D). At an angle of 60 degrees

Q 24. Chlorination of water is done for removal of ____________.

A). Bacterias

B). Suspended solids

C). Sediments

D). Hardness

Q 25. Removal of grease and oil from sewage is called _________.

A). Screening

B). Filtering

C). Skimming

D). Bypassing

Q 26. Which gas can cause explosion in sewers?

A). Carbon monoxide

B). Carbon dioxide

C). Methane

D). Ammonia

Q 27. The frame of a ratchet brace is shaped like the letter _________.

A). L,

B). C,

C). U,

D). O,

Q 28. Figure below shows three types of traps. Name them in order from left to right.

A). P - trap; Y - trap; S - trap,

B). P - trap; Q - trap; R - trap

C). L - trap; Q - trap; S - trap

D). P - trap; Q - trap; S - trap

Q 29. Figure below shows a drain pipe. The lowest point (marked 'B') of the drain pipe where the liquid is the deepest is called ____________.

A) Invert

B) Cleancut

C) Battery

D) Fall

Q30. When used in the context of plumbing, what does 'DWV' mean?

A) Drain-Waste-Vent

B) Dam-Water-Valve

C) Damp-Waste-Ventilation

D) Dry-Waste-Valve

Q 31. The tree system of water distribution ___________.

A). Is relatively costly

B). Has many valves

C). Makes determination of discharges and pressure difficult

D). Causes stagnation of water

Q 32. What is provided in elevated storage reservoir for circulation of air?

A). Overflow pipe

B). Float gauge

C). Ventilator

D). Manhole

Q 33. Name the water supply distribution system as shown in figure given below.

A). Dead end system

B). Radial system

C). Grid iron system

D). Ring system

Q 34. Axial flow centrifugal pumps are characterised by ___________.

A). High flow and low pressure

B). Low flow and high pressure

C). High flow and high pressure

D). Low flow and low pressure

Q 35. A number of plastic materials are used to manufacture pipes. Which material is of flexible type?

A). Polybutylene (PB)

B). Polyvinyl chloride (PVC).

C). Chlorinated polyvinyl chloride (CPVC).

D). All of these

Q 36. Which material is used for pipes which conduct waste?

A). Stainless steel

B). Copper

C). Ceramic

D). Plastic

Q 37. Which of these centrifugal pumps has the higher specific speed than others?

A). Axial flow

B). Radial flow

C). Mixed flow

D). All centrifugal pumps have same specific speed

Q 38. There are different methods of detecting leakge in pipelines. What method is being used as shown in figure given below?

A) By using electronic leak detector

B) By using sounding rod

C) By using radioactive isotopes

D) By visual inspection

Q 39. Which of these is an example of use of radio isotope to detect leakage?

A). Sodium 6

B). Sodium 12

C). Sodium 18

D). Sodium 24

Q 40. Figure given below shows that _______________.

A). Intensity of leak sound is directly proportional to water pressure

B). Intensity of leak sound is inversely proportional to water pressure

C). Intensity of leak sound is directly proportional to water pressure upto a limit

D). Intensity of leak sound is inversely proportional to water pressure upto a limit

Q 41. When the inlet pressure in a water pump falls below designed specification, what happens is shown in figure below. The process of formation and subsequent collapse of vapour bubles is called:-

A). Surge

B). Cavitation

C). Suction

D). Hammer

Q 42. The disposal of sewage from the septic tank is done by __________.

A). Clarifier

B). Soak pit

C). Aerated lagoon

D). Lamp holes

Q 43. Which of these valves is placed at dead end or lowest point in the mains and is provided to remove sand or silt deposited in the pipeline?

A). Scour valve

B). Reflux valve

C). Altitude valve

D). Sluice valve

Q 44. In case rain water is discharged into sewer, it is connected before ___________.

A). Manhole

B). Chamber

C). Gully trap

D). Bend

Q 45. A chamber of a large septic tank employing syphonic action to automatically discharge a large volume of effluent when a predetermined quantity has accumulated is:-

A). Drain field

B). Sewage treatment chamber

C). Seepage pit

D). Dosing chamber

Q 46. Figure below shows a cast iron bell-type cistern. It is painted inside with ___________.

A). White paint

B). Yellow paint

C). Black bituminous paint

D). Cream paint

Q 47. A pump with a mechanical seal has developed a leak at the gland. What could be the cause for this?

A). The pump packing has failed allowing water to drip out slowly

B). The pump ran dry ruining the seal faces

C). This is normal operation for mechanical seals

D). When the seal spring was installed, it allowed pressure between the two seal parts allowing water to leak out

Q 48. As the hot water heater tank is being filled up, you should ___________.

A). Clean it up

B). Purge the tank of air

C). Flush the toilet

D). None of these

Q 49. What is called the vertical distance of a column of water from the pump discharge?

A). Head loss

B). Friction head

C). Gravity head

D). Pressure head

Q 50. The non-soluble materials i.e. the end product after biological action of bacteria in waste and which settles at the bottom of the septic tank is called:-

A). Scum

B). Sledge

C). Sludge

D). Smudge

Q 51. The jelly like substance being formed in the process of coagulation is:-

A). Scum

B). Sledge

C). Floe

D). Alum

Q 52. For laying 100 mm diameter pipe, what should be trench width ('W' shown in figure given below) so as to ensure stable conditions?

A). 200 mm

B). 300 mm

C). 400 mm

D). 600 mm

Q 53. Which maintenance can be performed on a pump while it is running?

A). Lubricating impeller fins

B). Tightening packing nuts

C). Replacing seal parts

D). Replacing the packing

Q 54. For easy self-cleaning in sewer line, for a 150 mm diameter pipe, minimum gradient/slope should be:-

A). 1 in 25

B). 1 in 50

C). 1 in 75

D). 1 in 100

Q 55. Which of these is NOT a type of thermostat?

A). Bi-metallic type

B). Mercury expansion type

C). Electronic type

D). None of these

Q 56. A type of vegetation formed when water reservoir is exposed to light is called:-

A). Septic scum

B). Sledge

C). Pond scum

D). Floe

Q 57. In hot water system expansion/vent pipes are installed on the cylinder and boiler because they ____________.

A). Prevent air locks

B). Stop build up of lime

C). Supply cold water

D). Release excess steam and water

Q 58. When setting out a mechanical drawing in AutoCAD, what units should be set?

A). Fractional

B). Decimal

C). Architectural

D). Metric

Q 59. When drawing a line using the relative coordinate system a line is created from:-

A). 0, 0,

B). The ending point of last line

C). The beginning point of last line

D). None of these

Q 60. What joining compound is used to assemble PVC pipes with fittings?

A). Epoxy

B). Solvent cement

C). Glue

D). Spray adhesive

Q 61. The term used in the consturction industry to specify the installation of all pipes in a plumbing system, is:-

A). Roughing-in

B). Plumbing layout

C). Piping network

D). Piping works

Q 62. A pump which is used underground is ____________.

A). Reciprocating pump

B). Rotary pump

C). Submersible pump

D). Gear pump

Q 63. A piece of trim (marked 'A' in figure below) that covers the hole where the pipe penetrates the wall is called:-

A). Strap

B). Escutcheon

C). Strip

D). Flat

Q 64. The system of water distribution which is suited to a city growing irregularly is:-

A). Tree system

B). Radial system

C). Grid iron system

D). Ring system

Q 65. What is the test used in determining if a newly installed water system is leak proof?

A). Pressure test

B). Hydraulic test

C). Hydrostatic test

D). Pneumatic test

Q 66. Which type of pipe is used to crossing the road in the pipeline?

A). AC pipe

B). Brass pipe

C). C. I. Pipe

D). CCR pipe

Q 67. Which of the following is not a task performed by a plumber?

A). installing fan in bedroom

B). repairing sanitation system

C). fitting bathrooms

D) repairing water pipelines

Q 68. Dry powder fire extinguishers cannot be used for the fires generated due to______________.

A). cooking oils and fats

B). electrical equipments

C). flammable liquids

D). wood or paper

69. ______________are used to hold pipes for drilling operations.

A). V-blocks

B). Centre punch

C). Surface gauge

D) Hammer

Q 70. Which of the following hand tools delivers a blow to an object?

A). Hammer

B). Plier

C). Angle Plate

D) Chisel

Q 71. Identify the following masonry tool

A). Pickaxe

B). Shovel

C). Spade

D) Trowel

Q 72. Which of these devices determines perpendicularity in masonry?

A). Plumb bob

B). Spirit Level

C). Edger

D) Float

Q 73. In_____________position, a brick is laid flat with the short end of the brick exposed.

A). Header

B). Soldier

C). Sailor

D) Shiner

Q 74. Ordinary cement is also known as_______________cement.

A). Portland

B). Switzerland

C). Ireland

D). England

Q 75. Which of the following is used to cut external threads on cylindrical workpieces?

A). Threading Die

B). Ratchet Brace

C). Bit Brace

D). Pipe Wrench

Q 76. ___________are useful for seized joints.

A). Offset wrench

B). End pipe wrench

C). Rapid grip wrench

D). Chain pipe wrench

Q 77. The given picture depicts a_____________.

A). Box spanner

B). Adjustable wrench

C). Strap wrench

D). Torque spanner

Q 78. Class C pipe of GI pipes are marked in __________colour for identification.

A). red

B). blue

C). yellow

D) green

Q 79. CPVC pipes are ______________ductile as compared to PVC pipes.

A). more

B). less

C). equally

D) less or equally

Q 80. Which of the following piping symbol is depicted in the given symbol?

A). Vent line

B). Cold water line

C). Hot water line

D). Waste Line

Q 80. Cross fittings are also known as ____________fittings.

A). 4-way

B). 2-way

C). 6-way

D). 9-way

Q 82. Water is composed of_____________.

A). Oxygen and Hydrogen

B). Hydrogen and Chlorine

C). Chlorine and Oxygen

D). Helium and Oxygen

Q 83. Reverse Osmosis is a _____________process.

A). water purification

B). refrigerating

C). air conditioning

D). water impurification

Q 84. _________are provided at all dead ends to drain out waste water.

A). Blow-off valves

B). Stopcock

C). Plug cock

D). Needle valve

Q 85. The following figure represents a____________valve.

A). Ball

B). Ball check

C). Air relief

D) Air Inlet

Q 86. _____________water distribution system is suitable for old towns having no definite pattern of roads.

A). Tree

B). Radial

C). Grid

D) Ring

Q 87. In ____________ drainage system, all waste from washbasins, sinks, baths and WC waste is fed into a same large bore vertical system.

A) single stack

B) partially ventilated single stack

C) one pipe

D) two pipe

Q 88. Which of these occurs if a suction pressure develops in a drainage system?

A) Induced siphonage

B) Backpressure

C) Trap

D) Self-siphonage

Q 89. Which of the following statements is not TRUE regarding Cesspool?

A) It treats the waste water

B) It collects the waste water

C) It is located below ground level

D) It is covered with a manhole

Q 90. A choked toilet is often cleared using a __________________.

A) cooper's plunger

B) pump plunger

C) sink plunger

D) power plunger

Q 91. Identify the type of pump shown in the figure:

A) Rotary pump

B) Reciprocating pump

C) Centrifugal pump

D) Booster pump

Q 92. Axial flow centrifugal pumps are characterized by _________flow and _________pressure.

A) high, low

B) high, high

C) low, low

D) low, high

Q 93. What is the process of removing the trapped air from the pump and filling it completely with water?

A) Priming

B) Casing

C) Tapping

D) Boosting

Q 94. Symbol for which of the following options has been depicted below?

A) Pipe turns down

B) Water Heater shut off

C) Pipe turns up

D) Clean out

Q 94. Which of these is an outlet provided in water pipe particularly in case of fire?

A) Fire Hydrant

B) Stopcock

C) Water meter

D) Scour valve

Q 95. The post hydrant remains projected _____________above ground level.

A) 60 cm-90 cm

B) 10 cm-25 cm

C) 20 cm- 50 cm

D) 100 cm-150 cm

Q 96. MSP is an abbreviation used for________________.

A) Main Soil Pipe

B) Mini Soil Pipe

C) Mega Soil Pipe

D) Major Soil Pipe

Q 97. Which of the following is not a desirable property of trap?

A) Complexity in cleaning

B) Smooth internal surface

C) Self-cleansing

D) Easy to fix with drain

Q 98. Heat capacity of a body is expressed in____________.

A) joules per kelvin

B) joule kelvin

C) joules per second

D) joules per kilogram

Q 99. The outer surface of a glass having hot water is also hot. This is due to______________.

A) conduction

B) convection

C) radiation

D) dispersion

Q 100. Which of the following pipes connects the main supply from the water board to your house ?

A) Service pipe

B) Communication pipe

C) Supply pipe

D) Suction pipe

Q 101. In a central heating system, the diverter valve__________________.

A) switches the hot water flowing from boiler to radiator

B) heats hot water tank

C) turns the boiler on when heat is needed

D) provides programmed selection

Q 102. In unsealed roadways, the minimum trench depth for laying pipes should be____________.

A) 750 mm

B) 1000 mm

C) 450 mm

D) 300 mm

Q 103. Where a sewer line crosses road or a drain, it should be passed through_____________.

A) RCC pipe

B) Aluminium pipe

C) PVC pipe

D) GI pipe

Q 104. The given picture depicts _____________urinal.

A) Trough

B) Floor mounted

C) Bucket

D) Wall hung with P-trap

Q 105. The method of water treatment wherein denser objectionable elements settle on the bottom of the basin for easy separation, is ___________.

A). Filteration

B). Sedimentation

C). Straining

D). Setting

Level 2 Answer Key

Question No.	Option	Question No.	Option	Question No.	Option
1	B	44	C	87	A
2	C	45	D	88	A
3	D	46	C	89	A
4	B	47	B	90	A
5	B	48	B	91	A
6	C	49	D	92	A
7	B	50	C	93	A
8	D	51	A	94	A
9	B	52	C	95	A
10	A	53	B	96	A
11	C	54	D	97	A
12	C	55	D	98	A
13	B	56	C	99	A
14	D	57	D	100	A
15	D	58	B	101	A
16	D	59	B	102	A
17	C	60	B	103	A
18	D	61	A	104	A
19	B	62	C	105	B
20	D	63	B		
21	C	64	A		
22	C	65	A		
23	B	66	C		

24	A	67	A
25	C	68	A
26	C	69	A
27	A	70	A
28	D	71	A
29	A	72	A
30	A	73	A
31	D	74	A
32	C	75	A
33	C	76	A
34	A	77	A
35	A	78	A
36	C	79	A
37	A	80	A
38	B	81	A
39	D	82	A
40	C	83	A
41	B	84	A
42	B	85	A
43	A	86	A